I0802524

# Praise for *Jesus Felt It Too*

"*Jesus Felt It Too* inspires young women to become more self-aware leaders as they follow Christ's example of using emotions in an effective and righteous way."

—Dr. Susan R. Madsen
Women & leadership global thought leader, author, speaker, and professor

"Our Savior is a God of deep empathy, not mere sympathy. He not only atoned for us, but he felt with us as he experienced mortality. *Jesus Felt It Too* teaches this powerful truth in an engaging and novel way for children and youth. Whether they are feeling calm or anxious, abandoned or joyful, sad or thankful, they will learn that they can use any emotion to do good as Jesus did."

—Dr. Anthony Sweat
Author and professor of Church History and Doctrine at Brigham Young University

"I love how *Jesus Felt It Too* helps us clearly see how Jesus felt the full spectrum of human emotion. As a perfect person, He righteously used all of His emotions by doing good no matter what He was feeling. As you read *Jesus Felt It Too*, you will see the beauty of emotions and be inspired to use them in righteous ways!"

—Cali Black
Author, speaker, and scriptorian behind Come Follow Me Study

"Through easy-to-read stories, *Jesus Felt It Too* beautifully paints the full range of Christ's emotions–from joyful to anxious to sorrowful and more. This book's inspiring message will help you feel closer to Christ and leave you wanting to become more like Him as you work on using any emotion you feel to do good."

—Ben Lomu
Host of BYUtv's "Come Follow Up," actor, and religious educator

"*Jesus Felt It Too* is an exceptional resource that brings real human emotions to the front of gospel study. This book highlights the human-ness of Jesus Christ, helping us feel that He is relatable, that He does understand what we are feeling as we stumble along our mortal journeys. I highly recommend *Jesus Felt It Too*. I am thrilled to share it with my friends, family members, and clients as together we become more like Him."

—Tammy Hill
Licensed marriage & family therapist, educator, and author

"Understanding our emotions and the feelings of others is a hallmark of healthy development. *Jesus Felt It Too* is a fantastic resource for helping parents and children strengthen their spiritual development by learning about the wide variety of emotions Jesus felt during His mortal ministry."

—Dr. Peter Reschke
Professor in the School of Family Life at Brigham Young University and expert in emotional development

Text © 2024 Amber Corkin, Aubri Robinson, and Ashley LeBaron-Black
Artwork © 2024 Brooklynne Noe, Esther Hi'ilani Candari, Janelle Susan Cunningham, Jessica Beach, Lovetta Reyes-Cairo, Matt Harward, Meikah Carter, Mike Call, and Rebecca Jessee

All rights reserved.

No part of this book may be reproduced in any form whatsoever, whether by graphic, visual, electronic, film, microfilm, tape recording, or any other means, without prior written permission of the publisher, except in the case of brief passages embodied in critical reviews and articles.

The opinions and views expressed herein belong solely to the author and do not necessarily represent the opinions or views of Cedar Fort, Inc. Permission for the use of sources, graphics, and photos is also solely the responsibility of the author.

ISBN 13: 978-1-4621-4620-8
ebook ISBN 13: 978-1-4621-4666-6

Library of Congress Control Number: 2023951499

Published by CFI, an imprint of Cedar Fort, Inc.
2373 W. 700 S., Suite 100, Springville, UT 84663
Distributed by Cedar Fort, Inc., www.cedarfort.com

Cover artwork of Jesus by Esther Hi'ilani Candari
Cover and interior layout by Shawnda T. Craig
Cover design © 2024 Cedar Fort, Inc.

Printed in Columbia

10 9 8 7 6 5 4 3 2 1

Printed on acid-free paper

this book belongs to

For Johnny, who loves Jesus and is full
of beautiful, deep emotions.

—Amber

For Tom, my biggest supporter and best friend.

—Ashley

For my little man, Rocky. I'm excited to
watch you grow in wisdom and stature.

—Aubri

# JESUS FELT IT TOO

## BIBLE STORIES OF HIS EMOTIONS

written by AMBER CORKIN, AUBRI ROBINSON & ASHLEY LEBARON-BLACK

CFI • An imprint of Cedar Fort, Inc. • Springville, Utah

# contents

# artwork

# JESUS FELT EMOTIONS

The shortest verse in the Bible contains only two words: "Jesus wept" (John 11:35). Despite being short, this verse is packed with power. It boldly and quickly tells us that Jesus experienced deep emotions. Jesus lived a mortal life, growing in "wisdom and stature" and feeling emotions—just like you (Luke 2:52).

You feel a wide variety of emotions, like joy, anxiety, disappointment, surprise, curiosity, sadness, and confidence. Your emotions give your brain and body information. They help you understand the world around you.

Do you know that Jesus knows *exactly* how you feel? As part of His mortal life on earth, Jesus felt the full range of human emotion. Because Jesus is a perfect person, surely feeling emotions is good. Not only did Jesus experience emotions throughout His life, but through the Atonement He felt everything you have felt and ever will feel. Whatever you are feeling, you are not alone in that emotion. Jesus felt it too.

This book shares 28 different emotions that Jesus felt in the Bible. As you dive into these stories and consider the prompts that follow, you can learn about yourself through Him and see your divine potential.

# JESUS WENT ABOUT DOING GOOD

Emotions and feelings are only half of the story! Jesus felt *and* He "went about doing good" (Acts 10:38). He felt and then He acted.

Jesus experienced different emotions that helped Him turn outward and bless, heal, lift, and love others along the way. He continues to provide us with healing, comfort, and love. You can help others along your way too! Emotions can help you better relate to what others are feeling. Every day, there are opportunities to help and love the people around you.

*Feel* and *do*. You can do good no matter what you are feeling. As you experience emotions and as you go about doing good, you are becoming more like Jesus.

# JESUS FELT ABANDONED

There once was a place called Golgotha, which means "a skull." It was there that Jesus was taken to be crucified.

Naked and in pain from the tortures of soldiers, Jesus hung on a cross. Above His head was His accusation: "THIS IS JESUS THE KING OF THE JEWS."

Jesus was not the only one at Golgotha that day. Criticizing people passed by His cross, shaking their heads and insulting Jesus. They said that if He was the Son of God, like He claimed, He should be able to save Himself and come down from the cross. Priests, scribes, and elders stood by, mocking Him. Even two thieves, hanging on their own crosses to Jesus's right and left, insulted Him.

Not everyone witnessing the scene that day was critical; Jesus had loving supporters watching on, heartbroken by their Master's sufferings. These friends included His mother, His Apostles, and His followers who had witnessed Jesus teach, serve, and heal. Many women disciples were among those watching and supporting Jesus from afar.

Suddenly, a darkness covered the land. After three dark hours, Jesus cried with a loud voice saying, "My God, my God, why hast thou forsaken me?" Despite being surrounded by people, Jesus hung on His cross feeling alone and abandoned.

After Jesus cried out one last time, His spirit left His mortal body. The earth quaked and the people feared greatly and confessed, "Truly this was the Son of God."

## FEEL & DO

Why did Jesus feel abandoned? What is something good that Jesus did in this story? When have you felt abandoned? How can you do good when you feel abandoned?

Matthew 27:33–56; Mark 15:15–41;
Luke 23:35–38, 46–49; John 19:16–22, 25–27

# JESUS FELT ANGRY

One day, the Pharisees sat watching and waiting. They were a proud group of religious leaders who strictly followed and enforced their rules for the Sabbath day. Closely watching Jesus as He entered the synagogue, their place of worship, they hoped to catch Him breaking the law of the Sabbath.

Upon entering, Jesus saw a man with a withered hand. Jesus could heal him, yet the Pharisees did not allow healing on the Sabbath. Knowing in His heart what was the right thing to do, Jesus said to the man with the withered hand, "Stand forth."

Aware of the Pharisees' watchful eyes, Jesus turned to them and asked questions, hoping to soften their hearts. Was it better to do good or evil on the Sabbath? Was it better to save a life, or to kill? But the Pharisees were so set in their ways with hardened hearts that they stayed silent and watched on. Jesus "looked round about on them with anger, being grieved for the hardness of their hearts."

Although angry with the Pharisees, Jesus turned, focusing His loving attention on the man. Jesus asked him to stretch forth his withered hand. As he extended it, the man's hand was miraculously healed.

Immediately, the Pharisees went to tell the political leaders what Jesus had done, hoping to destroy Him. Having healed many, Jesus left the synagogue and traveled toward the sea. A great crowd followed Him, rushing to be healed of their sicknesses and plagues.

## FEEL & DO

Why did Jesus feel angry? What is something good that Jesus did in this story? When have you felt angry? How can you do good when you feel angry?

Matthew 12:1–15; Mark 3:1–10; Luke 6:1–19

# JESUS FELT ANXIOUS

Jesus anxiously awaited His approaching death. He knew that in just a few days He would be killed in one of the most painful ways possible: crucifixion.

Being vulnerable, Jesus admitted to His followers, "Now is my soul troubled." He continued, "And what shall I say? Father, save me from this hour"? Jesus could have pleaded with His Heavenly Father to spare Him from crucifixion, but He knew what He had to do. The reason He came to earth was to atone and die for us.

Instead of asking God to spare Him from pain and death, Jesus prayed aloud, asking for the glory to go to God. As soon as Jesus had spoken His brave prayer, there came a voice from heaven promising that God's name would be glorified. Some of His followers thought the voice was thunder; others thought it was the voice of an angel, but it was the voice of God.

Jesus may have continued to feel anxious as He courageously declared that He would soon die. He then gave this comforting promise to all of us: "I am come a light into the world, that whosoever believeth on me should not abide in darkness. . . . I came . . . to save the world."

## FEEL & DO

Why did Jesus feel anxious? What is something good that Jesus did in this story? When have you felt anxious? How can you do good when you feel anxious?

John 12:27–33, 46–47

MIKE CALL
2 0 2 3

# JESUS FELT BETRAYED

One evening, Jesus reclined around a table with His twelve Apostles. It was the last supper He would eat before His death. John, whom Jesus loved, rested his head on Jesus.

Troubled in spirit, Jesus revealed to His Apostles, "One of you shall betray me." Looking around in shock at each other, His Apostles wondered which of them could possibly betray their beloved friend and teacher. Devastated, they all cried, "Lord, is it I?"

Holding a piece of bread, Jesus answered that He would dip the bread in a dish and give it to the person who would betray Him. He said, "Woe unto that man by whom the Son of man is betrayed!" It would have been better for the betrayer if he had never been born. He dipped the bread and held it out to Judas Iscariot.

Indeed, Judas *had* been plotting to turn Jesus over to religious leaders who wanted Him dead. Judas asked, "Master, is it I?" Jesus responded simply, "Thou hast said."

Judas took the bread from Jesus, and Jesus told him to do it quickly. The other Apostles were confused and did not know what Jesus meant, but Judas immediately stood and hurried out into the night to find the religious leaders.

Jesus turned to His eleven faithful Apostles. He knew He would not be with them much longer. Tenderly calling them little children, He gave them a new commandment to love one another.

## FEEL & DO

Why did Jesus feel betrayed? What is something good that Jesus did in this story? When have you felt betrayed? How can you do good when you feel betrayed?

Matthew 26:19–25; Mark 14:16–21;
Luke 22:13–14, 21–23; John 13:1–2, 21–35

# JESUS FELT CALM

In a ship upon the sea of Galilee, Jesus sat facing a large crowd gathered along the seashore. He spent the day teaching them through stories. When evening came, Jesus and His disciples sent the multitude away.

Then, launching the ship from the shore, they began sailing across the large lake. Tired from His day, Jesus retreated to the rear of the ship, laid His head on a pillow, and fell fast asleep.

While Jesus slept, a great storm emerged. Fierce winds blew and raging waves beat against the ship. Soon the ship filled with water. Their lives were in danger! His disciples were greatly concerned by the situation. They desperately awoke Jesus and cried, "Master, carest thou not that we perish?"

Calmly standing, Jesus rebuked the winds and commanded the waves, "Peace, be still." The storm stopped and there was a great calm.

Turning to His disciples, Jesus asked, "Why are ye so fearful? Where is your faith?" In awe, the disciples wondered aloud about the miracle they had witnessed and the Prince of Peace, who had enough power that even the wind and water would obey Him.

## FEEL & DO

Why did Jesus feel calm? What is something good that Jesus did in this story? When have you felt calm? How can you do good when you feel calm?

Matthew 8:23–27; Mark 4:1–2, 35–41; Luke 8:22–25

# JESUS FELT COMPASSIONATE

In a city called Nain there lived a widow who only had one son. Sadly, one day he died. Devastated by her loss, the widow mourned greatly.

When the time came for the burial, her son's body was placed upon a stretcher so it could be carried to the gravesite outside the city gates. Weeping, the widow followed the stretcher that carried her precious son. Many people from the city walked with the mourning mother as they wound their way toward the place of burial.

During the funeral procession, Jesus approached the city with His disciples. Drawing near the gates, He saw the mourners and beheld the weeping widow. Moved with compassion, Jesus told her, "Weep not."

Coming to the stretcher, Jesus touched it, and those carrying the stretcher stopped and stood still. Full of empathy for the widow's sufferings, Jesus looked down upon her son's lifeless body and commanded, "Young man, I say unto thee, Arise."

Miraculously, the son sat up and began to speak. He was alive again! Jesus delivered him to his mother, and all who witnessed this wonderful scene glorified God.

## FEEL & DO

Why did Jesus feel compassionate? What is something good that Jesus did in this story? When have you felt compassionate? How can you do good when you feel compassionate?

Luke 7:11–16

# JESUS FELT CONCERNED

Mary, who was highly favored by God and blessed among women, willingly accepted her role as the mother of Jesus. She sacrificed much to bring Jesus into the world, birthing Him in a humble stable far from home. Protecting Him as He grew in wisdom and stature, Mary took care of her precious son and loved Him deeply.

Likewise, Jesus showed love and concern for His mother.

In His last moments of life, as He hung bleeding on a wooden cross, Mary stood nearby. She painfully watched on, supporting her firstborn son as He cruelly suffered. When Jesus saw His mother there, instead of being consumed by His own sufferings, He was filled with concern for her. Asking His disciple John to care for her, Jesus instructed, "Behold thy mother!" From that day on, John would take Mary into his own home and care for her.

Only after Mary was taken care of did Jesus know that His purpose on earth was accomplished and the scriptures were fulfilled. "It is finished," He said, bowing His head and giving up the ghost.

## FEEL & DO

Why did Jesus feel concerned? What is something good that Jesus did in this story? When have you felt concerned? How can you do good when you feel concerned?

Luke 1:26–38; Luke 2; John 19:25–30

# JESUS FELT CONFIDENT

One day Jesus spoke to an astonished crowd. It was the Sabbath, and Jesus had entered a synagogue, a building of worship, to teach the Jews. Unlike the scribes who merely memorized wise words and repeated them to the people, Jesus taught with confidence, power, and authority. The people were fascinated with His words and teachings.

Among the crowd was a man possessed by an unclean, evil spirit. The man yelled at Jesus, asking Him to leave them alone. Mocking Jesus, the possessed man asked what business He had with them and if He had come to destroy them.

As the crowd looked on, Jesus confidently commanded the evil spirit to come out of the man and depart. After the man foamed at the mouth, gnashed his teeth, and cried with a loud voice, the evil spirit finally left him. The man was healed.

Again, the crowd was amazed, questioning each other about who this man was, "for with authority commandeth he even the unclean spirits, and they do obey him." The news of Jesus and His power immediately spread throughout the land.

## FEEL & DO

Why did Jesus feel confident? What is something good that Jesus did in this story? When have you felt confident? How can you do good when you feel confident?

Mark 1:21–28; Luke 4:30–37

# JESUS FELT CURIOUS

One day twelve-year-old Jesus went missing. Every year His family joined a large caravan traveling from His home in Nazareth to Jerusalem for the feast of the Passover. For a week Jesus and His family ate special food, sang hymns, and prayed.

After the festival was over, Jesus's parents, Mary and Joseph, started the long walk back to Nazareth with the rest of the traveling group. They thought Jesus was walking with some of their extended family or friends. At the end of the day when the group stopped to rest, Mary and Joseph searched everywhere for Jesus, calling His name, but He was nowhere to be found. Frantically, they hurried as fast as they could back to Jerusalem to find their precious, lost son.

Finally, after three days of desperate searching, Mary and Joseph found Jesus in the temple. Feeling curious, Jesus had been deep in conversation with a group of teachers—listening carefully, asking questions, and answering questions Himself. Everyone at the temple was amazed at the wisdom of this twelve-year-old boy.

Mary likely hugged Jesus as she asked Him why He had run off like that. She and Joseph had been worried sick. Jesus responded by asking His mom why they had been looking for Him. Did they not know He had to go about His Father's business? Because God was Jesus's Father, Jesus had been in God's house, doing what God wanted Him to do.

Obediently, Jesus went back to Nazareth with His parents. Under their care, He continued to grow stronger and smarter.

## FEEL & DO

Why did Jesus feel curious? What is something good that Jesus did in this story? When have you felt curious? How can you do good when you feel curious?

Luke 2:41–52

# JESUS FELT DETERMINED

Covered in bruises and spit while wearing a crown of piercing thorns, Jesus was led away by Roman soldiers to Golgotha—the place where He would be crucified. A great company of women and men followed and watched, some weeping.

When they came to Golgotha, the soldiers gave Jesus a mixture of vinegar and gall, a drink typically given to ease the pain of a dying person. When the bitter liquid passed Jesus's lips for the first time, He recognized what it was and refused another drink. Jesus knowingly chose not to dull the pain nor His senses, for He was determined to experience the full suffering of His Atonement.

Jesus, the King of the Jews and Redeemer of all, was crucified between two robbers. He keenly felt the nails driven through the palms of His hands and wrists and the weight of His body pulling Him toward the earth. He clearly heard the weeping of His mother. He intently prayed to His Father in Heaven on behalf of those who caused His suffering.

Determined to fulfill His mission on earth, Jesus willingly suffered and was crucified atop the hill. He died according to prophecy and finished His earthly ministry.

## FEEL & DO

Why did Jesus feel determined? What is something good that Jesus did in this story? When have you felt determined? How can you do good when you feel determined?

Matthew 26:1–2; Matthew 27:26–55; Mark 15:16–37;
Luke 23:27, 32–47; John 19:1–4, 16–30

# JESUS FELT DISAPPOINTED

With only hours left on earth, Jesus spent His precious time with His Apostles. They ate, talked, and sang together in an upstairs room.

When the time came for them to depart into the night, they left the city, crossed a brook, and came to the Garden of Gethsemane that sat on the slope of the Mount of Olives.

Turning to His Apostles, Jesus said, "Sit ye here, while I shall pray." He took Peter, James, and John a little ways farther into the garden and asked them to wait and watch. Traveling alone about a stone's throw away, Jesus fell to the ground. He prayed to God, begging to be spared from what He knew was coming. Yet, He began to perform the unbearable task of taking upon Himself all of humanity's pains, sins, and sorrows. This act of love was so excruciating that He bled from every pore.

Concluding His prayer, Jesus returned to His Apostles and found that they were asleep. Disappointed, He said to Peter, "What, could ye not watch with me one hour?" After all He had done for His Apostles, why could they not help Him tonight? Again, He asked them to watch and pray.

Two more times Jesus returned to find His Apostles asleep again. With heavy eyelids, they surrendered to sleep instead of waiting and watching with Jesus when He desperately could have used their support. Finding them asleep a third time, Jesus said to them, "Sleep on now, and take your rest: it is enough, the hour is come." He would soon be betrayed by one of His own Apostles and taken to be crucified.

## FEEL & DO

Why did Jesus feel disappointed? What is something good that Jesus did in this story? When have you felt disappointed? How can you do good when you feel disappointed?

Matthew 26:26–30, 36–46; Mark 14:22–46;
Luke 22:19–21, 39–48; John 13:1, 30; John 18:1–7

# JESUS FELT DISPLEASED

On the coasts of Judaea, people came carrying their young children in their arms. Wanting their children to be blessed by the Messiah, they pushed through the crowd toward Jesus as He preached. Each one longed for their little ones to simply be touched by Him.

Scolding them, Jesus's disciples turned them away. Their Master was very busy, and these were just children.

When Jesus saw His disciples scolding the people, "he was much displeased." Wanting to bless the dear children, Jesus insisted that His disciples let the little ones come to Him.

He explained, "Whosoever shall not receive the kingdom of God as a little child, he shall not enter therein." Little children are humble and believing, as everyone should be. Just like children are fully reliant on their parents, everyone should fully rely on God.

After taking the precious children up in His arms, Jesus put His hands upon them and blessed them—each one special to Him.

## FEEL & DO

Why did Jesus feel displeased? What is something good that Jesus did in this story? When have you felt displeased? How can you do good when you feel displeased?

Matthew 19:1–2, 13–15; Mark 10:1, 13–16; Luke 18:15–17

# JESUS FELT EAGER

One day, the Apostles, Peter and John, were in search of a special room. Jesus had instructed them to enter the city of Jerusalem, find a man carrying a pitcher of water, and follow him to his home. They were to ask the man where Jesus might eat the Passover meal. Just as Jesus foretold, the man led the Apostles upstairs to a large, furnished room. There, Peter and John prepared for the Passover.

When the time came, Jesus and the other ten Apostles arrived and gathered in the upper room. This would be Jesus's last supper before His great sacrifice and death—His last chance to share an important moment alone with them. Jesus revealed, "With desire I have desired to eat this passover with you before I suffer."

Grasping a cup, He gave a prayer of thanks and said to His Apostles, "Take this, and divide it among yourselves." The drink was a symbol of His blood, "which is shed for you." Then, with unleavened bread in hand, Jesus gave a second prayer of thanks. Upon breaking the bread, He gave it to them and instructed, "This is my body which is given for you: this do in remembrance of me."

It would soon become clear why Jesus had so eagerly desired to have this experience with His Apostles. This sacred moment in that large, upstairs room was the first sacrament. It provided a special way for all to remember Jesus and His sacrifice.

## FEEL & DO

Why did Jesus feel eager? What is something good that Jesus did in this story? When have you felt eager? How can you do good when you feel eager?

Matthew 26:17–20, 26–29; Mark 14:12–18, 22–25; Luke 22:7–20

# JESUS FELT EMPATHETIC

In the city of Jerusalem near a sheep market was a pool of water called Bethesda.

Said to have healing powers, the pool attracted large crowds of desperate people waiting under its five covered porches. The blind, withered, and disabled anxiously watched for movement in the water. It was believed that an angel went down at a certain time into the pool and moved the water. Whoever stepped into the moving water first was healed of their ailment.

One day, Jesus was walking by and spotted a certain man lying near the pool. For thirty-eight years, the man had suffered from a disability and clung to the hope of being healed.

Jesus, knowing the helpless man had been waiting at the pool's edge for a long time, approached him and asked, "Wilt thou be made whole?" The man explained that he had no one to help him quickly enter the water. Every time the water moved, someone else stepped in before he could.

Full of empathy, Jesus knew the man's sufferings and longed to heal him. Jesus lovingly commanded, "Rise, take up thy bed, and walk." Miraculously, the man was immediately healed.

## FEEL & DO

Why did Jesus feel empathetic? What is something good that Jesus did in this story? When have you felt empathetic? How can you do good when you feel empathetic?

John 5:1–9

# JESUS FELT FORGIVING

One early morning, Jesus walked to the temple. The people there flocked to Him, so Jesus sat down and began to teach them.

Meanwhile, the scribes and Pharisees brought a woman to Jesus. They stood her in the middle of the crowd and accused her, saying, "Master, this woman was taken in adultery." There was no denying this woman had sinned greatly because she had been caught in the very act. She had broken a law of Moses, and the men knew the punishment for breaking this law was to be stoned, meaning rocks would be thrown at her until she was dead. The scribes and Pharisees, trying to trick Jesus into saying something wrong, asked Him what He thought they should do to the woman.

Stooping to the ground as if He had not heard them, Jesus began to write with His finger in the dirt. When the scribes and Pharisees pressed Jesus for an answer, He stood and spoke with forgiveness, saying, "He that is without sin among you, let him first cast a stone at her." Then He bent down and continued writing on the ground.

All who heard Jesus's answer felt guilty for judging a woman when they had their own sins and shortcomings. One by one, beginning with the oldest, they left. Finally, only Jesus and the woman remained.

When Jesus stood and saw that they were alone, He said to her, "Woman, where are those thine accusers? Hath no man condemned thee?" She said, "No man, Lord." To which Jesus replied with loving forgiveness, "Neither do I condemn thee: go, and sin no more."

## FEEL & DO

Why did Jesus feel forgiving? What is something good that Jesus did in this story? When have you felt forgiving? How can you do good when you feel forgiving?

John 8:1–11

# JESUS FELT JOYFUL

One day Jesus welcomed tax collectors and sinners into His home to eat. When the Pharisees and scribes, who thought they were more righteous than other people, saw Jesus sitting amidst His guests, they grumbled. How could He eat with such sinful people? Hearing their whispered complaints, Jesus told three stories.

The first story was about a lost sheep. If a shepherd had one hundred sheep and one was lost, the shepherd would leave the ninety-nine and go searching in the mountains for the one until he found it. The sheep would be lovingly carried home upon the joyful shepherd's shoulders. In celebration, the shepherd would gather his friends and neighbors, saying, "Rejoice with me; for I have found my sheep which was lost."

The second story was about a lost coin. If a woman had ten pieces of silver and lost one, she would light a candle and sweep the house, searching diligently. When the coin was found, she would rejoice.

The third story was about a lost son. If a father had a son who left home, foolishly wasted his money, and made bad choices, the father would continue to hope for his homecoming. When the son returned, humbled and ashamed of his sins, the father would recognize him from afar, run to him, joyfully embrace him, and fully forgive him. A party would be thrown in the son's honor, celebrating he who once was lost but now was found.

Jesus taught that like the lost sheep, coin, and son, people make mistakes and become spiritually lost. Of course He spent His time with sinners who had lost their way. As the Good Shepherd, He feels "joy . . . over one sinner that repenteth" and is found.

## FEEL & DO

Why did Jesus feel joyful? What is something good that Jesus did in this story? When have you felt joyful? How can you do good when you feel joyful?

Matthew 18:11–14; Mark 2:15–17; Luke 15; John 10:11

# JESUS FELT LOVING

On a special evening, the Master became the servant. Having just finished His last supper, Jesus stood, took a towel, and prepared for a tender moment with His twelve Apostles. Jesus knew that His time on earth was coming to an end. "Having loved his own which were in the world," Jesus wanted to perform a loving act of service for them, for He "loved them unto the end."

Jesus poured water into a basin and began washing the dusty feet of His Apostles, one by one. Lovingly, He wiped them with the towel.

When it was Peter's turn, he said to Jesus, "Thou shalt never wash my feet," for he was the servant and Jesus the master. Yet, Jesus gently persuaded him and Peter gratefully accepted.

As Jesus made His way through the twelve men, He came to Judas. Jesus knew that this friend and disciple who had been with Him for years would betray Him that night. Despite this, Jesus knelt and cleaned his feet, too.

After washing all of the Apostles' feet and sitting back down, Jesus taught them: If He, their Lord and Master, was willing to wash their feet, they should also wash the feet of others. The lowly act of washing their feet was a symbol. "I have given you an example, that ye should do as I have done to you," for the "servant is not greater than his lord." Jesus promised that as they followed His example and lovingly served others, they would be happy.

### FEEL & DO

Why did Jesus feel loving? What is something good that Jesus did in this story? When have you felt loving? How can you do good when you feel loving?

John 13:1–17

# JESUS FELT MEEK

One day, a prophecy was made: "Behold, thy King cometh unto thee, meek, and sitting upon [a donkey], and a colt." Hundreds of years later, this prophecy came to pass.

Approaching the city Jerusalem, Jesus sent two of His disciples into a nearby village. He told them they would find a donkey and a young colt tied up. After untying the animals, the disciples should bring them to Him. If anyone criticized their actions, they were to say, "The Lord hath need of them."

The disciples went and did as Jesus instructed. Sure enough, they returned with the donkey and colt. After they had draped their clothes on the colt, Jesus sat upon it and began meekly riding toward Jerusalem.

A very large crowd gathered. To show their respect for Jesus, people began to spread their clothes on the ground in His path, welcoming and honoring Him like a king. Others ran to cut down tree branches and reverently laid them along the road. Praising Jesus, everyone shouted, "Hosanna to the Son of David: Blessed is he that cometh in the name of the Lord; Hosanna in the highest."

This procession created such a commotion that all of Jerusalem buzzed, asking, "Who is this?" And the people replied, "This is Jesus the prophet of Nazareth of Galilee."

Despite all the bustle, Jesus fulfilled the prophecy by coming to Jerusalem quietly and gently. He came to atone and die for all humankind.

## FEEL & DO

Why did Jesus feel meek? What is something good that Jesus did in this story? When have you felt meek? How can you do good when you feel meek?

Zechariah 9:9; Matthew 21:1–11; Mark 11:1–11; Luke 19:28–40

# JESUS FELT PATIENT

One day Jesus received an urgent message: His friend Lazarus was deathly sick. Jesus knew that if He rushed to the town of Bethany, He could heal Lazarus, but Jesus waited. He also knew that if He was patient, He could help more people. Meanwhile, Lazarus got sicker and sicker and then died. After two days, Jesus declared to His disciples that now that Lazarus was dead, it was time to go.

Once in Bethany, Jesus wept. He loved His friend Lazarus. Despite His tears, Jesus knew an even greater miracle that would strengthen people's belief was now possible.

Surrounded by a crowd, Jesus approached Lazarus's tomb, a cave with a large stone sealing the entrance. Jesus commanded that the stone be removed. Martha, the sister of Lazarus, objected, worried the body would already stink. Reassuring Martha, Jesus promised that if she would just believe, she would see the glory of God. Speaking to His disciples, Jesus had said, "I am glad for your sakes that I was not there [to heal Lazarus so that] ye may believe."

The stone was rolled away, revealing the dark cave. Looking to heaven, Jesus prayed, "Father, I thank thee that thou hast heard me." He wanted to be sure that the onlookers knew it was God who gave Jesus His miraculous power. With a loud voice, Jesus cried, "Lazarus, come forth."

Suddenly, a man wearing graveclothes walked slowly out of the cave. His hands and feet were bound with strips of linen and his face was wrapped in cloth. It was Lazarus, alive again! Jesus was glad that He had been patient so that many were able to see the mighty miracle. As He foretold, many who witnessed the scene believed in Him from that day forth.

## FEEL & DO

Why did Jesus feel patient? What is something good that Jesus did in this story? When have you felt patient? How can you do good when you feel patient?

John 11:1–45

# JESUS FELT PROTECTIVE

In the town of Bethany, Jesus sat eating supper with some of His disciples in the home of Simon the leper.

It was then that one of His dear friends, a woman named Mary, came into the room carrying an alabaster box. Inside her box was spikenard, a very precious and expensive ointment. Opening the box, she poured out a pound of the precious ointment and anointed Jesus's head and feet. Reverently, she began wiping His feet with her hair. Soon the whole house was filled with the smell of the ointment.

Some of the people present were secretly angry that Mary had used such an expensive ointment on Jesus. One of those people was Judas Iscariot, the disciple who would betray Jesus for thirty pieces of silver. He said, "Why was this waste of the ointment made? For it might have been sold for more than three hundred pence, and have been given to the poor." Whispering together, some of those present criticized Mary and complained about her wastefulness.

Jumping to Mary's defense, Jesus told them to leave her alone. He said, "Why trouble ye her? She hath wrought a good work on me." They would always have poor people around that they could help, but He would not always be with them. Jesus protectively praised her, saying that her kind act would be remembered all over the world and would be spoken of for generations to come.

## FEEL & DO

Why did Jesus feel protective? What is something good that Jesus did in this story? When have you felt protective? How can you do good when you feel protective?

Matthew 26:6–13; Mark 14:3–9; John 12:1–9

# JESUS FELT SAD

One day, Jesus beheld the city of Jerusalem, and tears fell from His eyes.

He had spent much of His time in that city, walking its roads, visiting its temple, and ministering to its people. Within the walls of Jerusalem, Jesus had healed a lame man, witnessed a widow part with her two precious mites, and given sight to a blind man. He loved the people in Jerusalem and knew their potential. He saw the goodness inside the city. Nevertheless, He was sad because He knew what was coming.

As Jesus gazed upon Jerusalem, He mourned its unfulfilled potential—if those within the walls only knew the peace He could give them, they might be spared! Alas, Jerusalem's enemies would soon surround the city and destroy it. How sad Jesus was to know such a city as Jerusalem was wicked enough to fall. He knew that Jerusalem's enemies would level the city—not leaving one stone upon another—and kill the people inside.

With this knowledge weighing on Him, Jesus wept over Jerusalem. When Jesus was done weeping, He entered the city and made His way to the temple.

## FEEL & DO

Why did Jesus feel sad? What is something good that Jesus did in this story?
When have you felt sad? How can you do good when you feel sad?

Mark 12:41–44; Luke 2:22, 41–50; Luke 19:41–45;
John 2:13–25; John 5:1–9; John 7:28–29; John 9:1–12

# JESUS FELT SCARED

It was nighttime and the Mount of Olives was covered in darkness. Jesus had come to the limestone hill east of Jerusalem with His disciples following behind Him. Withdrawing from them to be alone, Jesus said, "My soul is exceeding sorrowful unto death: tarry ye here, and watch."

Jesus felt the heavy load He carried and knew what daunting, painful tasks lay ahead. This was the night that He would suffer greatly, be betrayed by one of His closest friends, and be crucified for the world. Scared, He fell to the ground and prayed, "Father, if thou be willing, remove this cup from me: nevertheless not my will, but thine, be done." Jesus did not want to suffer, but He was willing to.

An angel appeared from heaven to strengthen and comfort Jesus. In agony, Jesus prayed more intensely. So great was His suffering that blood rolled down His body like sweat.

And so, the final events of His life began. Though He was scared of what lay ahead, He gathered strength from heaven and willingly pressed on.

## FEEL & DO

Why did Jesus feel scared? What is something good that Jesus did in this story? When have you felt scared? How can you do good when you feel scared?

Mark 14:26–36; Luke 22:39–44; John 18:1

# JESUS FELT SORROWFUL

In the small village of Bethany on the slopes of the Mount of Olives, there lived three siblings: Mary, Martha, and Lazarus. All three were dear friends of Jesus. He loved them.

One day, Lazarus got very sick. Mary and Martha knew that Jesus, who was in a different city, could heal him, so they quickly sent word. However, by the time Jesus arrived in Bethany, Lazarus had already been dead for four days, his body now wrapped in graveclothes and sealed in a tomb.

Overcome with grief, Martha and Mary mourned at home surrounded by friends. When Martha heard that Jesus was approaching the village, she went out to meet Him and cried, "Lord, if thou hadst been here, my brother had not died. But I know, that even now, whatsoever thou wilt ask of God, God will give it thee." Jesus reassured her, "Thy brother shall rise again."

Rushing back home, Martha found Mary among the crowd of mourners, and whispered to her, "The Master is come, and calleth for thee." Mary immediately jumped up and ran to Jesus. When she saw Him, Mary was overcome with emotion. Falling to her knees at His feet, she sobbed that if He had been there, then her brother would not have died. As Jesus saw her weeping, "he groaned in the spirit, and was troubled." Overcome with sorrow, "Jesus wept." The onlookers exclaimed, "Behold how He loved him!"

## FEEL & DO

Why did Jesus feel sorrowful? What is something good that Jesus did in this story? When have you felt sorrowful? How can you do good when you feel sorrowful?

John 11:1–36

MIKE
2023

# JESUS FELT SURPRISED

One day a centurion—a commander in the Roman army—came to Jesus begging for help. His dear servant was sick and lying paralyzed at home, suffering terribly and about to die.

When Jesus offered to come to his house to heal the servant, the centurion voiced concern. He did not feel worthy to host Jesus beneath his roof, but he knew that if Jesus merely spoke the words, even from far away, his servant would be healed. As a commander of an army, the centurion understood the power of authority. Just like when he commanded his soldiers to do something and it was done, he knew that if Jesus commanded the servant to be healed, he would be.

"When Jesus heard it, he marvelled." Jesus was surprised because He was a Jew, and the centurion was a Roman. Many of the Jews and Romans did not get along because the Romans ruled over the Jews and forced them to pay taxes. Despite having authority over Jesus, the centurion came to Him for help. In addition, the Romans believed in their own gods and not the God of the Jews, so the centurion's belief in Jesus was all the more surprising.

Turning to His disciples, Jesus declared that among all of the Jews, He had never found anyone with as much faith as this Roman centurion.

Jesus told the commander to go home, and his servant would be healed—just as the commander believed he would be. Miraculously, the servant was healed that very moment.

## FEEL & DO

Why did Jesus feel surprised? What is something good that Jesus did in this story? When have you felt surprised? How can you do good when you feel surprised?

Matthew 8:5–13; Luke 7:1–10

# JESUS FELT THANKFUL

Near the sea of Galilee, Jesus went up into the mountain and sat among a large crowd of men, women, and children. Over four thousand people were gathered, and He healed many. Rejoicing, the people glorified God. They had seen the lame walk, the blind see, the deaf hear, and the dumb speak.

The people had followed Jesus for days with nothing to eat. Worried they would faint, Jesus refused to send them away hungry, but His disciples wondered where they would find enough bread to feed so many people. After Jesus asked them how many loaves of bread they had, the disciples searched and brought Him only seven loaves of bread and a few little fish.

Jesus was grateful for even the little they had. Commanding the crowd to sit on the ground, Jesus "took the seven loaves and the fishes, and gave thanks, and brake them." After offering His prayer of gratitude, Jesus gave the food to His disciples, who distributed them among the people.

Miraculously, every single person ate until they were filled. The disciples collected the leftover fish and ended up with seven baskets full. In Jesus's thankful hands, a few handfuls of bread and fish were enough.

## FEEL & DO

Why did Jesus feel thankful? What is something good that Jesus did in this story? When have you felt thankful? How can you do good when you feel thankful?

Matthew 15:29–39

# JESUS FELT UNSUPPORTED

Jesus traveled with His disciples near a city in northern Galilee at the bottom of a tall mountain. His death was fast approaching. Knowing this, Jesus wanted to prepare His devoted followers for the difficult events that lay ahead. He explained the need to travel to Jerusalem, where He would suffer immensely at the hands of the religious leaders. Although He would be killed after carrying the very cross He would be nailed to, Jesus promised that three days later He would rise again, resurrected.

Peter, His chief Apostle, loved Jesus and did not want to hear that his friend would soon be killed. Taking Jesus aside, Peter began scolding Him, telling Jesus that He was wrong and would not die.

Feeling that Peter's critical words were unsupportive of His divine mission, Jesus replied, "Get thee behind me, Satan: thou art an offence unto me." Rather than focusing on eternal things of God, Peter was focusing on temporary things he wanted. Jesus saw the bigger picture. He needed to die for us so that He could be resurrected, making it possible for all people to be resurrected after death.

Turning to all of His disciples, Jesus reminded them that to truly follow Him, they needed to deny their selfish desires and symbolically take up their own crosses. By losing their lives in Jesus's work and focusing on the things of God, they would find meaningful lives and be rewarded eternally.

## FEEL & DO

Why did Jesus feel unsupported? What is something good that Jesus did in this story? When have you felt unsupported? How can you do good when you feel unsupported?

Matthew 16:13, 21–27; Mark 8:27, 31–38

# JESUS FELT UPSET

There once was a beautiful stone temple in Jerusalem. The temple was a holy place for Jews and Gentiles to pray and worship God. From the time He was a child, Jesus visited the temple regularly, learning and teaching the gospel and likely having sacred experiences there.

But this time when Jesus entered the holy temple, He found that it had been turned into a busy marketplace. People were loudly exchanging money and selling oxen, sheep, and doves. To make matters worse, these money exchangers and merchants were being dishonest, taking advantage of those who came to worship God. Jesus felt upset seeing the temple defiled—no longer a quiet place of devotion for the people. Accusing them, He said, "My house is the house of prayer: but ye have made it a den of thieves."

Jesus began cleansing the temple. Binding cords together, He made a whip and directed the oxen and sheep out of the temple. He "overthrew the tables of the moneychangers," scattering the coins across the floor. Then, overturning "the seats of them that sold doves," He ordered them to take their animals and leave. Protective of God's house, Jesus would not allow anyone to conduct business within its walls. With the beautiful stone temple now cleansed, people once again came to pray and worship in peace.

## FEEL & DO

Why did Jesus feel upset? What is something good that Jesus did in this story? When have you felt upset? How can you do good when you feel upset?

Matthew 21:12–14; Mark 11:11, 15–17; Mark 12:35; Luke 2:42–49; Luke 19:45–47; John 2:13–16; John 7:14; John 8:2; John 10:23

# JESUS FELT WITHDRAWN

There once were two cousins, John and Jesus, born just months apart. They both came to earth with special missions to fulfill and shared a unique bond even before they were born. When they were in their mothers' wombs, baby John leapt for joy when he knew his cousin was close by.

Living in the desert, John ate locusts and honey and dressed in camel's hair. Although his lifestyle was simple, John's mission was important: to testify that Jesus was the Son of God and to prepare the way for Him. He preached the gospel and baptized those who believed in Jesus. He even baptized Jesus in the Jordan River.

Meanwhile, a wicked, powerful queen named Herodius wanted John dead, so she hatched an evil plan. During her husband Herod's grand birthday party, she sent her daughter to dance in the banquet hall. Pleased with the dancing, Herod promised to give the girl anything she wanted. At her mother's request, she replied, "Give me . . . the head of John the Baptist." Herod groaned because he knew John was a holy man, but he could not break his word. Immediately, an executioner was sent to behead John, and the evil queen was pleased.

The devastated disciples buried John's body and hurried to tell Jesus. Upon hearing the horrific news of His cousin's death, Jesus felt withdrawn. Wanting to be alone and escape the crowds, "he departed thence by ship into a desert place apart" to rest and grieve privately.

However, a multitude followed Jesus on foot and were there waiting for Him to come ashore. After taking the time to lovingly heal, teach, and feed the people, Jesus sent the multitudes away. Finally, "he went up into a mountain apart to pray: and when the evening was come, he was there alone."

## FEEL & DO

Why did Jesus feel withdrawn? What is something good that Jesus did in this story? When have you felt withdrawn? How can you do good when you feel withdrawn?

Matthew 3:1–17; Matthew 11:7–11; Matthew 14:3–23; Mark 1:2–11; Mark 6:17–47; Luke 1:5–80; Luke 3:1–22; Luke 7:24–29; Luke 9:9–18; John 1:6–36

## ________ FELT

Write your name, current emotion, and story in the spaces provided. Include why you are feeling that emotion, what you can learn, and how you can use your experience to bless, lift, and love others.

### FEEL & DO

Whatever you are feeling, know that Jesus has felt it too. Just like Him, you can choose to do something good no matter what emotion you experience. As you feel emotions and go about doing good, you are becoming more like Jesus.

Draw a portrait or insert a photo of yourself here.

# acknowledgments

The emotion we are feeling right now is immense gratitude for our amazing support system. Thank you to our children and niblings (aka nieces and nephews) for inspiring this book with their big emotions and love for Jesus. Thank you to our husbands—Jake, Nathaniel, and Tom—for their unwavering love and encouragement. Thank you to our #1 fan (also known as Mom). Thank you to our nine wonderful illustrators who expertly captured the many emotions of Jesus. Thank you to our editor, Kaylee Mason, for dealing with our typoes (haha) and to Cedar Fort for helping to make this book a reality. Thank you to our readers of all ages who keep coming back for more. Most of all, thank you to Jesus Christ, who is our strength, our song, and our salvation.

# artists

## BROOKLYNNE NOE

Brooklynne Noe is a Southern-born mom and illustrator who recently survived her first Idaho winter. She has loved reading and illustrating stories all her life and is honored to help share these very important stories of our Savior. @brooklynnedraws

## ESTHER HI'ILANI CANDARI

Esther Hi'ilani Candari is an Asian American artist from Hawai'i who explores unique concepts such as multiracial identity; gender and the female gaze in the context of religion; and the connections between ecology, culture, and an important sense of place in her everyday work. @hiilanifinearts

## JANELLE SUSAN CUNNINGHAM

Janelle Susan Cunningham has always had an immense love for art and paints during her small breaks from motherhood in her Colorado home. She is inspired by the beauty of flowers, the strength of motherhood, and Christ's unconditional love in our lives. @janellesusanart

# artists

## JESSICA BEACH

Jessica Beach's work is inspired by her faith in Jesus Christ and inner pensive ploddings. Through digital illustration she shows overlooked beauty in life and the mirth of our mortal mileage. She creates the whispering of "Carpe Diem" she has heard from other artists' works. @jessicabeach143

## LOVETTA REYES-CAIRO

Lovetta Reyes-Cairo is an artist and mother working from her home studio in Utah. Her work is both personal and universal, often featuring the human figure and exploring ideas of motherhood, spirituality, and love. @lovettareyescairoart

## MATT HARWARD

Matt Harward is a husband, father, artist, and art teacher living in Huntington Beach, CA. He loves the outdoors and being with his family. The gospel of Jesus Christ helps him to stay positive in the midst of life's challenges. @mattharwardart

# artists

## MEIKAH CARTER

Meikah Carter is an artist currently based out of Virginia. Life, God, her family, and the works of others inspire her to create thoughtful pieces which include topics of religion, every-day life and her own original works of fiction. @makings.by.meikah

## MIKE CALL

Mike Call is an artist and educator living in Northern Utah. He studied art at Ricks College and at the Lyme Academy College of Fine Arts. You can find his art is in public and private collections across the globe. @mikecallfineart

## REBECCA JESSEE

Rebecca Jessee is an oil painter based in Holladay, UT. She studied illustration at BYU and now paints out of her home while she raises her busy little family. @beccajessee

# *authors*

## AMBER CORKIN

As a passionate writer and speaker, Amber Corkin has co-authored the award-winning book *Dear Divine Daughter: Inspiring Stories of Bible Women*, the study journal *Divine & Here to Shine*, and *Dear Divine Daughter: Inspiring Stories of Women in Latter-day Scripture*. Her children's book *Willow Wants a Wart* highlights the themes of body positivity and self acceptance. Amber loves chasing lofty goals, like that one time she bicycled coast-to-coast across the U.S. She lives in St George, Utah with her husband and three little kids.

## ASHLEY LEBARON-BLACK

Dr. Ashley LeBaron-Black is an Assistant Professor of Family Life at Brigham Young University where she teaches family theory and family finance. She received her PhD in Family Studies and Human Development from the University of Arizona. Her research focuses on money management in romantic relationships and how parents teach children about money. Ashley has published over 50 peer-reviewed papers and is an Associate Editor for the *Journal of Family and Economic Issues*. She is Chair of the Family Financial Wellbeing focus group for the National Council on Family Relations (NCFR). Ashley and her husband Tom live near Provo, Utah.

authors

## AUBRI ROBINSON

Aubri Robinson is creative, friendly, and resilient. From her local church in Minnesota to the United Nations in Geneva, Switzerland, she has volunteered as an advocate for girls and women. She is the co-author of *Dear Divine Daughter: Inspiring Stories of Bible Women*, *Divine & Here to Shine*, and *Dear Divine Daughter: Inspiring Stories of Women in Latter-day Scripture*. Aubri has four cherished children and is madly in love with her husband, Nathaniel. With a degree in business strategy, Aubri owns a branding and website design company and has done creative work for top brands like Samsung®, Silk®, and Puddle Jumper®. As a type-1 diabetic with a passion for helping others, Aubri is pursuing graduate studies in healthcare.

# JESUS FELT IT TOO